95 Phonics Core Program™
Student Workbook
GRADE 2

VOL
a

95%
GROUP LLC ®

Copyright ©2020 by 95 Percent Group, LLC
Author: Susan L. Hall, EdD
First Edition
ISBN 978-1-935853-98-5
PH4002.05
847-499-8200
www.95percentgroup.com
Printed in the United States of America
9   10   11   12   13   14   15   16   17

R3.10.22

Passage 1

Flin and Stef

1 Flin and Stef are two black lab pups who like to make a mess. They are
2 small pups, but the mess they make is big. When Brock takes them for a walk,
3 they pull away to find the mud. Once Flin steps in the mud, Stef jumps up and
4 down and runs after him.
5 After Brock grabs the pups from the mud and skips up the steps of his
6 home, Mom yells, "Stop!" Flin and Stef skid to a stop. Mom asks Brock, "Can
7 you help? They must get a bath." The pups run away and hide from Brock.
8 Brock knows that once he finds them and puts them in the tub, they will make
9 a mess again. Soon, the two pups come back and plop in the bath. They slip
10 from the suds and slop the mud on the wall and the sides of the tub. "What
11 a mess!" whines Brock.
12 Mom puts the pups out so they don't drip on the beds and rugs. Soon,
13 Flin and Stef get a sniff of Prim, the cat. Prim is the boss and she likes to play
14 tricks on the pups. She snaps at the pups and jumps on them when they trot
15 by her. Flin and Stef don't like it when Prim plays tricks on them. They run to
16 Mom for help. Mom snaps at Prim to stop bugging the pups. Prim gives a hiss
17 and runs away.
18 Now that Prim has run to hide and the mud is washed away, the small
19 pups can plop down on the steps to nap. Flin and Stef are two glad labs!

Passage 2

The Red Fox Pack

1   The red fox is big and like a wild dog. It runs with a pack. A fox pack can

2   be named a skulk. They hunch in packs of five to six in dens to be safe and help

3   block the chill after the sun sets. A red fox can run fast. With a quick dash, the

4   red fox can block his tracks, which will stop a clash with a wild cat. The red fox

5   is so quick that you could miss one if you look away too soon.

6   The red fox can see as well as a cat. This helps them catch lunch. A red

7   fox hunts and eats rats, bugs, and fish. A fox chomps on the bugs and fish for a

8   snack. A fox will catch frogs to eat too. Frogs are a big lunch for a fox. The fox

9   will bring the frogs back to the den so the fox pack can eat.

10   A small fox is a pup. The mom and dad are with the pups in the den.

11   The pups play in a bunch by the brush of the den so that the mom and dad

12   can see them. The brush and the quick steps of the pack will help them be

13   safe. You can look for the pups in the den but don't be shocked by mom and

14   dad standing by. It is best to see the red fox when it is big and not when it is a

15   little pup.

DAY 1

Sort Words

Word List				
1. led	3. sled	5. gloss	7. rim	9. smock
2. lip	4. clip	6. gob	8. trim	10. mock

Consonant Blends	NO
trap	rap
trim	led
sled	gob
gloss	rim
clip	lip
smock	mock

Sound-Spelling Mapping

c	l	i	p	

1. | f | l | a | t | |

2. | t | r | i | p | |

3. | s | t | o | p | s |

4.

5.

6.

7.

DAY 2

Pattern and Contrast Words

Word List				
1. hen	3. chip	5. rip	7. stamp	9. cash
2. flag	4. lock	6. then	8. hot	10. clip

Consonant Blends	Consonant Digraphs	NO
trip	chip	hen
flag	then	rick
stamp	cash	hot
clip	lock	Hotip

Sound-Spelling Mapping

p.	l.	o.	t.		

1.
m	ar	th			

2.
S	h	a	g		

3.
C	r	a	sh		

4.

5.

6.

7.

Read Passage — Passage 1
Go to page 2 and read *Flin and Stef*.

Written Response

Flin and Stef don't like it when ___taked a Bath___

DAY 3

Sound-Spelling Mapping with Student Phonics Chips

s.	m.	a.	sh.		

1.	f.	e	ll.			

2.	c.	r.	a.	B.		

3.	S.	h.	i	ff		

4.						

5.						

6.						

DAY 4

Fluency: High-Frequency Words

has	round	once	thank
open	tell	stop	again
may	going	pull	fly
sit	give	they	live

Sound-Spelling Mapping with Student Phonics Chips

ch	i	ll			

1.

2.

3.

4.

5.

6.

DAY 5

Number of Sounds in High-Frequency Words

Word List	
1. sit	4. once
2. pull	5. of
3. may	6. after

2 Sounds	3 Sounds	4 Sounds
	tell	

Fluency: Words

fuss	when	wish	kiss
class	math	trash	trap
flash	duck	buzz	snack
chat	shin	crash	hill

Fluency: Phrases

tell the twin	quick as a fox	fill with gum	fish with a net
pass the dish	the skunk stunk	trip the trap	flip the stack
good at math	a black clam	crack the whip	pull the sled
kiss the frog	the blue dress	sit on the hill	quack of a duck

Sentence Dictation

1._____

_____

2._____

_____

3._____

_____

Read Passage — Passage 1
Go to page 2 and read *Flin and Stef*.

Written Response

1. What made Mom yell?

_____

_____

2. What did Prim do to bug the pups?

_____

_____

 ## Read Passage — Passage 2
Go to page 3 and read *The Red Fox Pack*.

Written Response

1. List two facts from *The Red Fox Pack*.

_____

_____

_____

2. What are pups?

_____

_____

Passage 1

My Sis Is the <u>Best</u>

1 I have a sis, and she is the <u>best</u>. Well, I have three, and they are not like
2 the <u>rest</u>. I like to say we are the ABC kids. The "A" sis is Ann. She can be <u>strict</u>
3 and likes to be the boss of us. She is on a <u>quest</u> to tell us how to do a <u>task</u>. We
4 like to put her to the <u>test</u> when we do not <u>help</u> with the <u>tasks</u>. Ann will <u>scrunch</u>
5 her nose and <u>act</u> like she is mad. But we <u>trust</u> that her <u>rant</u> will not <u>last</u>.

6 The "B" sis is Bess. She is the sis at the top of the <u>list</u> with <u>zest</u>. She likes to
7 have a <u>blast</u> and can be a <u>pest</u>! Bess <u>sulks</u> if we don't want to play with her.
8 We do not like to <u>see</u> Bess sad, so we <u>split</u> up to play with her. Ann and I <u>loft</u> a
9 ball to Bess and she grabs it and <u>rolls</u> it back. Ann and Bess like to run fast and
10 <u>sprint</u> to the <u>swing</u> and back. To have a sis to play with is a gift.

11 Cam is sis "C." She is the sis who likes to rest and not <u>stress</u>. Cam finds
12 a spot to get <u>lost</u> and <u>drift</u> off for a nap when the sun sets. When Cam takes
13 a nap, <u>Bess</u> thinks it is fun to <u>pelt</u> her with buds from the plants and grass. This
14 wakes Cam and then we <u>all</u> <u>squint</u> and give a big grin at the fun we have
15 had.

16 I think I have the best <u>luck</u> to have my sis, all three, by my side. The ABC
17 kids are such a gift.

Passage 2

How to Craft a Drum

1   Drums are a blast to play. It is a fact that you can make a drum from stuff

2   at home. There are three drums that you can craft from things at home. This is a

3   fun, fast task.

4   You can craft a drum with a pot for the base. Find a cloth that will stretch

5   over the rim to make the top. The lid from the pot is the best top, but you may

6   risk a dent when you bang on it. Shift the crafted drum to a desk and test it out.

7   A big tin can with a scrap of rag will make a good drum. Trim a scrap of

8   rag to fit over the top of the can for the drum skin. The scrap must hang down

9   one inch from the top. Use a strip of duct tape to strap the scrap to the can.

10   The duct tape acts like a belt to hold the drum skin to the base.

11   To make the last drum, you must have a box. You can ask for a box from

12   a shop. Tape all sides of the box well. To make a strap to hold the box at the

13   neck, get a strand of string. Cut two holes in the top of the box and pull the

14   string in the holes. You may have to ask for help to hold the box still when you

15   twist the string in the holes.

16   All that is left to do is play the drums. You can play a drum with lots of

17   things. Just hunt for stuff in the home that will act like sticks. You will be glad

18   you spent time crafting a drum. Have fun!

DAY 1

Sort Words

Word List				
1. pat	3. past	5. left	7. wept	9. wet
2. let	4. rap	6. strap	8. best	10. bet

Consonant Blends	NO
scrub	rub
past	pat
left	let
strap	rap
wept	wet
best	bet

Sound-Spelling Mapping

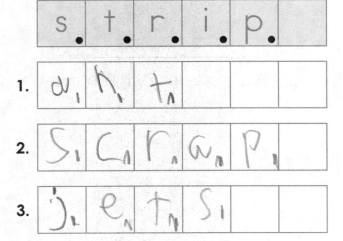

s.	t.	r.	i.	p.	

1. | a | h | t | | | |

2. | s | c | r | a | p |

3. | j | e | t | s | |

4. | | | | | | |

5. | | | | | | |

6. | | | | | | |

7. | | | | | | |

DAY 2

Pattern and Contrast Words

Word List				
1. fact	3. fat	5. lit	7. rat	9. raft
2. lift	4. belt	6. bell	8. sit	10. split

Consonant Blends	NO
gasp	gap
fact	fat
lift	lit
belt	bell
raft	rat
split	sit

Sound-Spelling Mapping with Student Phonics Chips

h	e	l	d		

1. | f | e | l | t | | |

2. | th | e | f | t | | |

3. | s | t | r | w | m | |

4. | | | | | | |

5. | | | | | | |

6. | | | | | | |

Syllable Mapping

First Syllable	Second Syllable	Word
ad	mit	admit
1. Pig	Pen	Pigpen
2. Swn	Set	Swnset

📄 Read Passage – Passage 1
Go to page 10 and read *My Sis Is the Best*.

Written Response

Ann can be _____ and likes to be the boss.

DAY 3

Sound-Spelling Mapping with Student Phonics Chips

b	l	a	s	t

1. | b | e | l | t | |

2. | s | t | r | a | p |

3. | m | a | th | |

4. | f | r | i | zz | |

5.

6.

7.

8.

9.

DAY 4

Fluency: High-Frequency Words

wash	both	sit	best
fly	going	could	fast
let	walk	pull	again
stop	tell	may	wish

Word Chains

must
mast
mass
mask

DAY 5

Number of Sounds in High-Frequency Words

Word List	
1. both	4. wish
2. fast	5. by
3. wash	6. how

2 Sounds	3 Sounds	4 Sounds
		best

Fluency: Words

kept	crisp	slept	help
chest	wilt	fact	cost
script	scrub	belt	must
gift	splash	best	tent

Fluency: Phrases

scrap the plan	with a flat raft	past the glass	on the soft dress
get the best plum	pass the gift	on a hunt	down by the camp
help with the quilt	a fun fact	a dash of salt	scrub the lift
grab the strap	the best plan	split the rent	craft the drum

Sentence Dictation

1. _____

_____

2. _____

_____

3. _____

_____

Read Passage — Passage 1
Go to page 10 and read *My Sis Is the Best*.

Written Response

1. Which sis is like you? How?

_____

_____

2. Who do you think is the big sis? What makes you think that?

_____

_____

 ## Read Passage — Passage 2
Go to page 11 and read *How to Craft a Drum*.

Written Response

1. Which drum do you think will make a big bang? How do you know?

_____

_____

_____

2. What could you use for drum sticks?

_____

_____

Passage 1

Tank and the New Kitten

1 My black lab, Tank, is my best pal. I have not had Tank long, but I think

2 Tank ranks as my best dog yet! He and I like to go on long walks at dusk. I fling

3 on my things as Tank sits next to me and longs for our walk.

4 I put a strap on Tank so that he will be safe. Tank could run into bad things,

5 like a fox gang, if he is not with me. The fangs of a fox could cut Tank if it bites

6 him. Tank could eat grass that hangs by the path. Too much grass could make

7 him ill. I don't want him to be unwell.

8 There are times when Tank will yank on the strap to stop and sniff things.

9 Yet, on this walk, Tank will not stop sniffing by the bank of the path. With a strong

10 yank, he pulls me down the bank into the long grass. Soon, a soft whine comes

11 from the grass. I fling back the grass to see a little yellow kitten.

12 "Come on, Tank," I say. "It's time to go." Tank will not come. I give a yank

13 to his strap, but he will not come. He sits by the kitten and whines. The kitten licks

14 Tank's nose.

15 "OK, Tank. You win. We will take the kitten home with us," I say. "But when

16 we redo this walk, we will not bring kittens home with us."

Lesson
3

Passage 2

Ball Games

1   There are games that <u>call</u> for a <u>ball</u> to play. In one game, you toss the

2 <u>ball</u> over the plate, and a pal will take a swing with a bat. The pal wants to hit

3 the <u>ball</u>. It takes three strikes to get the pal out. A home run is when the <u>ball</u>

4 is hit over the <u>wall</u>. You can <u>stroll</u> the bases when this happens. There are two

5 things that can let you <u>walk</u> to the base. One is when four <u>balls</u> go over the

6 plate. This is <u>called</u> a <u>walk</u>. Two, if a pitch is a <u>balk</u>. Both give you time to <u>walk</u>

7 to the base. These are not good in this <u>ball</u> game and can end in a loss. What

8 is the name of this <u>ball</u> game?

9   The next game is played with a black and white <u>ball</u>. You <u>unroll</u> a net

10 and connect it to two posts with bolts. You kick the ball into the net. You bolt

11 after the ball. In this ball game, there is not time to walk. This can take a toll on

12 the legs. The object of this game is to kick the most <u>balls</u> into the net to win the

13 game. What is the name of this ball game?

14   The last game has a small white ball. There is a club you hold to swing at

15 the ball. You can't talk when a pal swings. The object of the game is to get the

16 ball to the small hole in the grass called a cup. You have to hold still to make a

17 bold shot to win the game. There are times when you can play a hole again to

18 see who wins. What is the name of this ball game?

19   Can you think of some games that call for a ball? You can take a poll

20 to find out which game all the pals like <u>best</u> and host a <u>ball</u> game at home.

Lesson 3

DAY 1

Sort Words

Word List					
1. bring	3. clang	5. shrink	7. fang	9. long	11. pink
2. prank	4. zonk	6. swing	8. bonk	10. rank	12. strong

ang	ing	ong
sprang	Bring	long
clang	Swing	srong
fang		

ank	ink	onk
thank	shrink	Zonk
Prank	Pink	Bonk
rank		

Sound-Spelling Mapping

s .	t .	r .	ing	.

1. | S | oh9 | |
| | | |

4. | | |

2. | Ch | e | S | t |
3. | S | t r | ink |

5. | | |
6. | | |
7. | | |

Morphology

Notes About Prefixes			
Prefix	**Meaning**	**Prefix + Word**	**Meaning and Sentence**
re-	a9ain BacK	replay	to Play a9ain
			I like tha song anD I want to replay in.
un-	hot oppasite of	wnlock	

Prefix + Word	Meaning of Word
1. (re)read	to read a9ain
2. (un)tied	opposite or tieD hot tied

Lesson 3

DAY 2

Sort Words

Word List				
1. small	3. walk	5. told	7. sold	9. roll
2. jolt	4. most	6. wall	8. stalk	10. volt

old	olt	ost
told	jolt	most
sold	volt	

all	oll	alk
small	stroll	walk
wall	roll	stalk

Sound–Spelling Mapping

s	t	alk

1. F. old
2. S. t. all
3. S. t. alk

4.
5.
6.
7.

Writing: Contractions

2 Words	Combine Words and Slash Letters	Contraction
can not	can~~no~~t	can't
1. I am	I~~a~~m	I'm
2. could not	coul~~d~~~~no~~t	couldn't
3. did not	did~~no~~t	did'nt

Read Passage — Passage 1
Go to page 18 and read *Tank and the New Kitten*.

Written Response

The kitten licks _____

_____

Lesson 3

DAY 3

Pattern and Contrast Words

Word List			
1. grin	3. grind	5. chill	7. fine
2. child	4. find	6. mild	8. bind

 ild	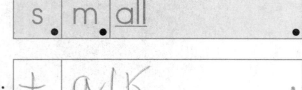 ind	 NO
wild	grind	grin
child	find	chill
mild	bind	fine

Sound-Spelling Mapping

s •	m •	all •

1. | t • | alk • |

2. | g • | r • | ind • |

3. | s • | g • | r • | a • | p • |

4.

5.

6.

7.

Phonograms

DAY 4

Fluency: High-Frequency Words

could	fast	wish	cold
some	call	sit	pull
wash	tell	going	sing
put	both	how	best

Syllable Mapping

	First Syllable	Second Syllable	Word
	pic	nic	picnic
1.	con	nect	conect
2.	wh	pack	whoack
3.	kit	en	kiten
4.			
5.			

Lesson 3

DAY 5

Number of Sounds in High-Frequency Words

Word List		2 Sounds	3 Sounds	4 Sounds
1. when	4. open	how		
2. why	5. may			
3. must	6. give			

Fluency: Words

old	crank	sting	troll
most	walk	stall	kind
hang	bolt	bonk	wild
long	stalk	gold	jolt

Fluency: Phrases

the kind child	a long walk	under the sink	just a ring
with a jolt	into the wild	from the song	with the king
over the gold	on a roll	had a ball	hang the blinds
bang the gong	find the tank	thank the host	bring the drink

Sentence Dictation

1. _____

_____

2. _____

_____

3. _____

_____

Read Passage – Passage 1
Go to page 18 and read *Tank and the New Kitten*.

Written Response

1. What could make Tank unwell on the walk?

_____

_____

2. What did Tank do after he sniffed the bank by the path? What made him do that?

_____

_____

_____

 ### Read Passage – Passage 2
Go to page 19 and read *Ball Games*.

Written Response

1. What three games are in *Ball Games*?

_____

_____

2. What are two things that make these three games the same?

_____

_____

_____

Passage 1

At the Lake

1   We woke up and ran down the steps as the sun rose. Mom said, "Let's

2   take a ride to Pine Lake. We can have a picnic at the lake." Drake and I yelled,

3   "Yes!" Gabe was not going to the lake with us. He said, "You can bring a pad

4   to take notes. Tell me what you saw when you get home."

5   Mom, Drake, and I drove to the lake. As we got to the lake, there was a

6   splash! I said, "Mom, it's a duck!" Drake made a note on the size of its neck. I

7   made a note that the duck was white with a black bill. We went to take a close

8   look. There were cute, little ducks tucked in close to the big one. We saw the

9   big duck wade in the shade. Mom said, "She will find fish there for these little

10   ducks to eat."

11   We kept going and came to a wide glade. A glade is a spot with open

12   land. Drake and I liked the glade, so we chose a spot to take a bite of the

13   snacks Gabe had made. Soon it was time to go home.

14   On the ride home, Drake and I had time to discuss our notes. We made

15   a list of the things we liked while at the lake. Once home, we ran to talk to

16   Gabe. As we spoke, he looked at our notes. We had notes on the ducks at

17   the lake and the glade where we ate. He said, "By this list, I see that you had

18   a fine time at the lake!"

Passage 2

Twigs from a <u>Vine</u>

1   I <u>like</u> <u>grape</u> <u>vines</u> to <u>make</u> crafts. You can <u>make</u> a craft with the twigs that

2 twist out from the <u>vines</u> where <u>grapes</u> hang. Once you <u>take</u> all the <u>grapes</u> from

3 the <u>vine</u>, it is <u>time</u> to <u>prune</u> the twigs you want for this craft. <u>Prune</u> is the <u>name</u> of

4 what you do when you <u>make</u> a cut.

5   Step one is to round up and <u>prune</u> the twigs from the <u>vine</u>. Put <u>these</u> twigs

6 in <u>piles</u> by <u>size</u>. This will help you <u>while</u> you <u>make</u> a craft hanging. You can <u>make</u>

7 a craft hanging in a ring <u>shape</u>. A bit of <u>wire</u> will <u>make</u> a good ring <u>shape</u>.

8   One trick I do <u>while</u> I <u>make</u> this craft is to <u>come</u> up with twigs that are not

9 too <u>wide</u>. <u>Wide</u> twigs are too stiff to bend well. You can bend the twigs into

10 the <u>shape</u> you want. If they snap when you bend and twist them, you can wet

11 them until they bend. Then, you can shape them while they are wet. Twist and

12 bend the twigs over the wire ring. Add twigs over these, bending them like a

13 hose and tucking in the ends.

14   The twigs from a vine of grapes will fade to a fine shade of brown over

15 time. You can add little rose buds to this hanging to make it pretty. I like to

16 make crafts from grape twigs. I hope you, too, will save twigs and make a craft.

Lesson 4

DAY 1

Sort Words

Word List				
1. tote	3. tube	5. grape	7. gripe	9. prune
2. eve	4. stroke	6. these	8. mate	10. stripe

ā	ē =	ī	ō	ū
grape	theme	kite	tote	tube
mate	eve	gripe	stroke	prune
	these	stripe		

Sound-Spelling Mapping

h	o	m			
.	.	e			

1. | B | r | a | ss | | |

2. | t | a | p | e | | |

3. | th | e | se | | | |

4. | | | | | | |

5. | | | | | | |

6. | | | | | | |

7. | | | | | | |

Lesson
4

DAY 2

Pattern and Contrast Words

Word List				
1. note	3. not	5. ate	7. shack	9. hit
2. a	4. at	6. she	8. hi	10. shake

Closed	Long Vowel Silent-e	Open
note	hote	no
at it	ate	a
Hit	shake	she
shak		Hi

Sound-Spelling Mapping with Student Phonics Chips

sh a k e

1.

2.

3.

4.

5.

6.

Lesson 4

 Read Passage – Passage 1
Go to page 28 and read *At the Lake*.

Written Response

They chose a spot in the _____
to take a bite of the snacks.

DAY 3

Sound-Spelling Mapping with Student Phonics Chips

sh.	e.				

1. | S | t | a|k | | |

2. | f | i | Ve | | |

3. | W | e | | | |

4.

5.

6.

Syllable Mapping

First Syllable	Second Syllable	Word
fab	ric	fabric
1. Cat	nap	catnap
2. nap	kin	napkin
3.		
4.		
5.		

DAY 4

Fluency: High-Frequency Words

write	both	cold	made
wish	call	tell	sit
sing	wash	five	pull
gave	fast	best	why

Word Chains

shake
take
wake
woke

stripe	made	Luck	
strip	mad	Lake	
trip	nat	Like	
rip	nate	pike	

Lesson 4

DAY 5

Fluency: Words

plate	like	hi	slope
prize	go	grade	home
these	flute	while	theme
strike	Pete	he	cute

Fluency: Phrases

he did smile	gave the theme	up the slope	write the tune
with a rake	she got the prize	for a while	on the drive
go to the game	go with me	in the vase	made the cake
why the note	they said take five	the cute home	save the grebe

Sentence Dictation

1. We saw the grebes Dive for Fish
   It's wnllike to st.. t..sm

2. It is whliike to Steve to not Smile

3. _____

Read Passage — Passage 1
Go to page 28 and read *At the Lake*.

Written Response

1. Why did the kids bring a pad to the lake?

_____

_____

2. What did Mom say the big duck would do when it went to wade in the shade?

_____

_____

 Read Passage — Passage 2
Go to page 29 and read *Twigs from a Vine*.

Written Response

1. What kind of twigs do you use for the craft?

_____

_____

2. What helps to make the ring shape?

_____

_____

Passage 1

A Goblin in the Attic

1   Just as I <u>drifted</u> off, <u>banging</u> from the attic woke me up. I <u>jumped</u> from

2   my bed and ran to Mom. As I <u>landed</u> on her bed, I <u>asked</u>, "What is that

3   <u>banging</u> in the attic? I think it could be a goblin!"

4   "What <u>banging</u>?" <u>asked</u> Mom. "I think you are <u>making</u> up this goblin so

5   you can nod off here with me. Go back to bed." I was <u>shocked</u>! How could

6   Mom shrug off the banging?

7   I skipped back to my bed, pulled up my socks, and hopped under my

8   blanket. The banging had ended. I dozed off, less upset that there could

9   be a goblin. I woke up again, this time to scratching. The scratches were

10   from the attic. Again, I landed on the bed next to Mom. "Mom, the goblin is

11   scratching now!" I was yelling as I woke her.

12   "What scratching?" asked Mom. "There is no scratching in the attic."

13   "Mom, I just know there is a goblin up there. Will you go and check it

14   out?" I begged. Mom got out of her bed and walked to the steps that go up

15   to the attic. She hiked up the steps and went into the attic. I was frantic that

16   the goblin would get Mom.

17   Mom stopped at the top of the steps and gave me a big grin. "I have

18   the goblin," she said as she picked up our tomcat to give to me. What a

19   mess! "Now, I am going back to bed, and you are not going to wake me up

20   again." I think I spotted a smile on her lips as she passed by me.

Passage 2

Insect <u>Bites</u>

1   Dusk is the time when the sun is just <u>setting</u> and the time when an insect

2 <u>comes</u> out from <u>hiding</u>. It would be a (mistake) to be out <u>walking</u> and <u>riding</u> <u>bikes</u>

3 if you don't want to be bitten by an insect. <u>Bugs</u>, <u>flies</u>, and <u>ants</u> are the <u>kinds</u> of

4 <u>insects</u> that will bite.

5   <u>Insects</u> will bite when they are upset. They (dislike) it when we sit next to

6 them and when we stroll by the <u>homes</u> they dwell in. <u>Ants</u> will often bite <u>us</u>

7 when we step on the <u>hills</u> they made. You do not have to be outside to be

8 bitten by a fly. They can get in our <u>homes</u> and bite <u>us</u> there.

9   When they sting and itch, insect <u>bites</u> can be very bad. I dislike getting

10 bit. You can stop <u>bites</u> by getting an object that zaps <u>insects</u>. Some do not

11 want to kill <u>insects</u>, so they use netting that <u>stops</u> them. By washing with <u>smells</u>

12 that the <u>insects</u> dislike, you can stop them from bugging you.

13   It will soon be cold and the <u>bugs</u>, <u>flies</u>, and <u>ants</u> will go away and not

14 upset you. They will be back again in the spring, so do not dispose of the things

15 you <u>used</u> to not be bitten by an insect.

DAY 1

Sort Words

Word List				
1. shave	3. check	5. chime	7. brunch	9. froze
2. click	4. we	6. by	8. pro	10. frost

Closed	Long Vowel Silent-e	Open
	stripe	my
click	shave	we
check	chime	by
brunch	froze	pro
frost		

Morphology

Notes About Word Endings			
Rule	**Verb**	**Verb + Ending**	**Spelling Rules**
1	wish	wishes wishing wished	Verbs **ending with ch, sh, s, x, or z**, add -es, -ed, or -ing.
2	bake	bakes baking baked	Verbs spelled with the **silent-e pattern, drop the last e** before adding -ing, -es, or -ed.
3	shop	shops shopping shopped	Verbs spelled with **1 vowel followed by 1 consonant, double the final consonant** before adding -ing or -ed. When adding -s, don't double the consonant.
4	cry	cries crying cried	Verbs spelled with a **consonant followed by y at the end, drop the y and add an i** before -es or -ed. When adding -ing, don't drop the y.

1. _____

_____

2. _____

_____

3. _____

_____

Lesson 5

DAY 2

Sound-Spelling Mapping

| b | r | o | k | e | |

1. | l | h | ch | | | |

2. | p | r | i | se | | |

3. | d | h | r | r | t | |

4. | s | p | y | | | |

5. | u | se | | | | |

6. | m | a | ke | s | | |

7. | sh | e | | | | |

Morphology

Word List
1. filled
2. asked
3. walked
4. drifted
5. begged
6. landed
7. shocked
8. ended
9. dozed

3 Pronunciations for -ed		
-ed = /ed/	-ed = /d/	-ed = /t/

Read Passage – Passage 1
Go to page 36 and read *A Goblin in the Attic*.

Written Response

There was _____ and _____ coming from the attic.

DAY 3
Morphology

Notes About Prefixes			
Prefix	**Meaning**	**Prefix + Word**	**Meaning and Sentence**
dis-	not, apart		to hot like something my dad dislikes Hot Dog
mis-	not, bad, wrong		to spell spell something wrong

Prefix + Word	Meaning of the Word
1. disagree	to hot agree
2. misread	to read something wrong
3. disband	to hot bond together to come apart
4. misuse	
5. misplace	

Syllable Mapping

	First Syllable	Second Syllable	Word
	rep	tile	reptile
1.	Bit	ten	Bitten
2.	in	sect	Insect
3.	con	fuse	confuse
4.			
5.			

DAY 4   1 2 3 4 5

Fluency: High-Frequency Words

call	write	very	both
would	sing	why	pull
made	five	again	your
going	every	cold	gave

Word Chains

bake	Strip	Hop
baking	Stripe	Hope
biking	Stripes	Hopes
bike	Striped	Hoped

Morphology

Word List
1. bugs
2. bats
3. wishes
4. ducks
5. lunches
6. waves
7. sniffs
8. misses
9. songs

3 Pronunciations for -s and -es		
-s = /s/	-s = /z/	-es = /ez/
bats	bugs	wishes
ducks	waves	lunches
sniffs	songs	misses

DAY 5

Fluency: Words

blame	so	brushes	jumped
cry	rides	driving	pro
talking	lifted	sitting	wish
mistake	dislike	dismiss	misled

Fluency: Phrases

the crying pups	would you mind	closed the lid	why the mistake
your last call	riding our bikes	your five dresses	asked the pro
both the songs	it is unsafe	dislikes the flies	rename the file
a very hot dish	skipped the line	could you try	landed the plane

Word Building

Word Part Bank		
Prefixes	**Base Words**	**Endings**
un	print	s
re	fill	es
dis	lock	ed
mis	use	ing

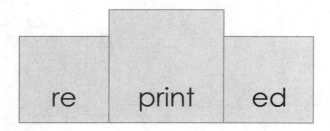

re print ed

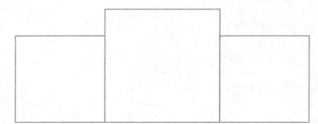

Sentence Dictation

1. _____

_____

_____

Read Passage — Passage 1
Go to page 36 and read *A Goblin in the Attic*.

Written Response

1. What did Mom find in the attic?

_____

_____

2. At the end, why do you think Mom smiled as she passed by the kid?

_____

_____

 ### Read Passage — Passage 2
Go to page 37 and read *Insect Bites*.

Written Response

1. What is one thing you can do to stop from getting bit by a bug?

_____

_____

2. Lines 14–15 said, "do not dispose of the things you used." What is "dispose"?

_____

_____

Passage 1

<u>Roaming</u> <u>Goat</u>

1   The big <u>goats</u> saw <u>Joan</u>, a small <u>goat</u>, <u>loafing</u> in the grass by the old

2   <u>oak</u>. <u>Joan's</u> <u>goal</u> was to <u>roam</u>, but they said she was too small to <u>roam</u>. <u>Joan</u>

3   liked <u>soaking</u> up the sun, but she could not stop thinking of the <u>sights</u> that

4   <u>might</u> be over the hill. She asked Buck <u>Goat</u> to let her <u>roam</u> to the big <u>oak</u> on

5   top of the hill.

6   The trip up the hill was the most fun Joan had in a long time! She could

7   see sights over the hill from the big oak. The sunlit sky was bright and the grass

8   so soft. She saw lights on the road down the hill. The things roaming the road

9   made her frantic. She ran home to Buck Goat and asked what the lights and

10   roaming things might be. He spoke of traffic lights and trucks on the roads.

11   At night, Joan was thinking of when she might get to roam again. She

12   wanted to munch the grass and see the lights on the roads. Joan saw Toad

13   as he croaked and hopped next to the oak. Toad was roaming and Joan

14   wanted to go too. Joan went roaming over the hill with Toad, hoping she

15   might see the sights. Toad and Joan went down the hill and Toad jumped out

16   on the road. Lights were flashing and trucks were roaming the roads.

17   Toad crossed the road, but Joan moaned and said it was time for bed.

18   She ran over the hill past the big oak to Buck Goat and gave a big sigh.

19   Roaming was fun, but Joan was glad to be home for the night.

Passage 2

A Toad's Life

1   Do you think it <u>might</u> be fun to be a <u>toad</u>? Let's find out what the life of

2 a <u>toad</u> <u>might</u> be like.

3   You can find <u>toads</u> from <u>coast</u> to <u>coast</u>. <u>Toads</u> like <u>soaking</u> on the banks

4 of ponds and lakes. It is a <u>sight</u> to see <u>toads</u> <u>floating</u> on big pads in ponds and

5 lakes. <u>Toads</u> do not like the cold and can get a <u>slight</u> chill. Some <u>toads</u> hop out

6 to soak up shafts of light in the sunlit sky. A toad out under the sunlit sky might

7 not sit too long. Too long in the hot sun will roast the toad's skin.

8   Toads connect at night on land. Toads roam to hunt. They see well in dim

9 light and go hunting for bugs and grubs on land. If a bug in flight lands by a

10 toad, it will soon slide down the toad's throat. It is sad to say, but some toads

11 get hit on the road while roaming at night.

12   At night, all toads will croak. Male toads croak the most when looking

13 for a mate. When they croak, you see the toad's throat go up and down.

14 The croak of toads may be in tune, like a song! At times, you might think the

15 croaking toads will not let you doze. To stop the croaking, you would have to

16 take baskets of toads away.

17   Do you admit it might be fun to be a toad? Could you be coaxed into

18 being a toad?

DAY 1

Sort Words

Word List				
1. coach	3. fight	5. bright	7. oak	9. soap
2. toad	4. loan	6. night	8. tight	10. might

igh	oa
sigh	throat

Sound-Spelling Mapping

	n	igh	t		

1.

2.

3.

4.

5.

6.

7.

DAY 2

Pattern and Contrast Words

Word List				
1. flight	3. clock	5. rode	7. boat	9. groan
2. light	4. road	6. sight	8. right	10. site

igh	oa	NO
	cloak	

Sound-Spelling Mapping with Student Phonics Chips

b.	r.	igh.	t.	

1.

2.

3.

4.

5.

6.

Read Passage – Passage 1
Go to page 46 and read *Roaming Goat*.

Written Response

Joan wanted to see _____

_____

DAY 3

Syllable Mapping

	First Syllable	Second Syllable	Word
	com	pete	compete
1.			
2.			
3.			
4.			
5.			

Morphology

Word Bank				
play	twist	hop	walk	float

1. (verb + -ing) _____

_____

2. (verb + -ed) _____

_____

DAY 4

Fluency: High-Frequency Words

write	would	cold	your
sit	pull	both	sing
best	made	five	call
very	its	gave	right

Word Chains

oat
coat
boat
bloat

Writing

Possessive and Plural Possessive			
Noun		**Possessive**	**Sentences**
Singular	pig		
Plural	pigs		

DAY 5

Fluency: Words

right	flight	boat	soak
road	fright	night	high
groan	sigh	coach	throat
slight	roam	croak	might

Fluency: Phrases

the frogs will croak	after the winning goal	the bright light	a foaming coast
all night long	by the tall oak	at the right time	in the shining cloak
with a sigh	has strep throat	the croaking toad	yelled with fright
go get my coat	with all his might	with a big groan	going to take flight

Sentence Dictation

1._____

_____

2._____

_____

3._____

_____

Read Passage – Passage 1
Go to page 46 and read *Roaming Goat*.

Written Response

1. The big goats said Joan was _____ to roam.

2. What were the lights and the roaming things on the road?

_____

_____

 ### Read Passage – Passage 2
Go to page 47 and read *A Toad's Life*.

Written Response

1. Male toads croak the most when they are _____

2. What helps toads hunt in dim light?

_____

_____

Passage 1

Bees at Deep Creek

1   The sun was hot as I used my <u>hoe</u> to plant <u>seeds</u> in the land. The <u>seeds</u>

2   would soon be plants. I was hot and <u>needed</u> to rest so I went to <u>Deep Creek</u>.

3   I sat on the bank under a <u>weeping tree</u>. The <u>weeping tree</u> has branches that

4   hang down that make it look like it is crying. The <u>weeping</u> branches were

5   <u>sweeping</u> in the wind. The wind felt good on my <u>cheeks</u>. I rested on my back

6   with my feet in the green grass.

7   The swishing of the sleek, running creek put me in a deep sleep. I did

8   not see the bee that landed on my toes. I woke up when I felt a prick on my

9   big toe. Well, the bee stung me while I was sleeping! I did not expect this

10 to happen. I wanted to keep sleeping next to Deep Creek, but my toe was

11 throbbing. I peeked at my toe and saw it swell. My toe was beet red!

12 I felt the buzz of bees sweeping by me as I sat up. They seemed upset

13 that I was under the tree. I looked up into the weeping tree and saw the

14 bees peeking at me from the hive. There were a lot of bees and they were

15 making a run for me. Yikes! I needed to get away from these foes unless I

16 wanted to contend with getting stung again.

17 I left Deep Creek and went back to my hoe. My sleep now over, it was

18 time to get back to planting seeds.

Passage 2

Feeling Good Feet

1   We need our feet to have a good life. Our feet take us where we need

2 to go. Our feet can speed at times. We can also creep on our toes. Some feet

3 are pretty and sleek. Some feet look bad with peeling skin. We must commit to

4 keeping our feet sleek.

5   We have 52 small bones in our feet from the heel to the tip of the toes.

6 We have fat pads on the soles of our feet, keeping them safe on the go. The

7 bones in our feet split into five toes. The big toe has two bones and the rest of

8 the toes in our feet have three bones.

9   We need to tend to our feet so they go on feeling good. Take time to

10 see how your feet look and feel. If you are on your feet too long, they will feel

11 pinched. Stubbing toes can make you weep and make toes bleed. We must

12 insist on keeping our feet from getting scraped and scratched. You have to

13 admit, your feet need socks. When you go out to get socks, plan to shop for

14 ones that will keep your feet from slipping. Slips are foes to feet, and you can

15 get a cracked bone. Cracked bones in feet do not feel good.

16   Our feet can get hot, and hot feet stink! Wash your feet by getting them

17 wet and scrubbing your toes. Dry your feet and toes and put on socks to keep

18 them smelling sweet. Feet do a lot for us, so don't object to keeping your feet

19 feeling good.

Lesson
7

DAY 1

Sort Words

Word List				
1. bleed	3. toes	5. feel	7. week	9. Joe
2. foe	4. beet	6. woe	8. hoe	10. tree

ee	oe
cheek	doe

Sound-Spelling Mapping

th	r	ee			

4.

1.

5.

2.

6.

3.

7.

DAY 2

Pattern and Contrast Words

Word List				
1. greed	3. goes	5. toe	7. woes	9. sweep
2. chess	4. tote	6. seem	8. swept	10. hoed

ee	oe	NO
teeth		

Sound-Spelling Mapping with Student Phonics Chips

f	ee	l			

1.
2.
3.

4.
5.
6.

Read Passage — Passage 1
Go to page 54 and read *Bees at Deep Creek*.

Written Response

The toe_____after the bee sting.

DAY 3
Syllable Mapping

	First Syllable	Second Syllable	Word
	pub	lic	public
1.			
2.			
3.			
4.			
5.			

Morphology

Notes About Prefixes			
Prefix	Meaning	Prefix + Word	Meaning and Sentence
fore-	before, earlier, at the front		
pre-	before, earlier		

DAY 4

Fluency: High-Frequency Words

right	sleep	your	call
made	tell	five	gave
green	why	around	would
its	don't	write	very

Word Chains

see
seek
sleek
sleep

Morphology

Prefix + Word	Meaning of Word	Sentence
1. foresee		
2. prebake		

Lesson 7

DAY 5

Fluency: Words

feel	foe	seem	doe
queen	goes	speech	Joe
toes	freed	woes	green
sweet	need	hoed	bleed

Fluency: Phrases

the soft green grass	right on my cheek	away from the queen	the free feeling
over the week	after they met Joe	go down three roads	around the creek
don't stub a my toe	black and white goat	on the green reef	float on a raft
went to greet Moe	a look of glee	goes to the wall	the speed boat

Sentence Dictation

1. _____

_____

2. _____

_____

3. _____

_____

Read Passage — Passage 1
Go to page 54 and read *Bees at Deep Creek*.

Written Response

1. Why did the kid need to rest?

_____

_____

2. Why were the bees upset?

_____

_____

Read Passage — Passage 2
Go to page 55 and read *Feeling Good Feet*.

Written Response

1. List two facts from *Feeling Good Feet*.

_____

_____

2. Why do we have fat pads on our feet?

_____

_____